Life Between the Questions

Carolyn Huffman

Illustrations by LuAnn Barrow

WORD BOOKS
PUBLISHER
WACO, TEXAS
A DIVISION OF
WORD, INCORPORATED

To Chuck —

Who loves me too much
to allow me to bury my gifts —

6.

Life Between the Questions

Often I ponder,
Sometimes I pray,
Over making lifes choices
As I use up my day.

8.

9.

Sometimes I ponder
The meaning of stars,
The destiny of man —
Will he travel to Mars?

Will Big Brother computers
Control our lifestyles?
Will my days be increased
By jogging those miles?

Is the atmosphere changing?
Will sea levels hold?
Will science cure cancer
Or diseases of old?

How do bees make sweet honey
In an intricate comb?
How do birds navigate
And find their way home?

14.

Who gave the canary
His rare singing throat
To rhapsody others
Without reading a note?

Why do chickens have feathers
And ducklings wear down?
Why do owls fly at night
With a funny hoot sound?

Why do chameleons change color
And camels grow humps?
Why are snails slippery, slimy?
What causes the mumps?

Just what makes a diamond?
Can you really train fleas
To dance and to tumble?
Why do things freeze?

Who programmed the piglets
To oink and to wallow?
Who gave Capistrano
Its claim to the swallow?

What makes the grass green
And the lightning bugs flicker?
Why do some folks get well
While others get sicker?

19.

20.

And why do some children
Grow gently with grace
While others bring chaos
To reign in a place?

Must all faces wrinkle
And all hair turn gray?
Must we always have winter?
Can't springtime just stay?

Why are tropics so hot
And arctic lands cold?
Why are some spinning hay
while others spin gold?

Who orchestrates lightning
To caper and prance
And calls forth the thunder
To follow the dance?

Turtles and olive trees
Keep living on.
Do you think this quite fair
To the rest of the throng?

Will nuke bombs explode
To blow us away?
Will any survive
To see one more day?

25.

26.

And what of the family
Who really believes
In a God of creation
Who loves, not deceives?

Some say, "Be a Buddhist!"
Others say, "Jew."
Some claim to be Muslim,
And others, Hindu.

Is there knowledge and truth
In the Christians' great claim
That Christ makes a difference
In playing life's game?

"Will life ever be fair?"
 Cries man to the sages.
"Unequivocally no,"
 Resounds through the ages.

30.

What about suffering
By the good and the bad?
Will I ever find answers
When I cry and am sad?

Or is that the right time
Not to ponder, but pray,
And to ask for the courage
To live one more day?

For questions don't matter,
And facts grow quite stale,
When life's storms surround you
Or wind drops from your sail.

Who really does care if
Brash science is right
When you're lost in a tunnel
of darkness, no light?

33.

You can fondle philosophy
And argue until
A loved one is hurt
Or lies dangerously ill.

Then, you fall to your knees,
And you pray with great might
For healing's soft touch
As you wait the long night.

When death marches through
And snatches a friend,
Your cry bombards heaven:
"Is this really the end?"

You can ponder on that one
Ten years and a day,
But the answers elude you...
Quit pondering and pray!

36.

38.

Let prayer be your mainstay,
A disciplined thrust.
God's reality will brighten,
And so will your trust.

Pondering is natural.
Men will always ask why
The good have to suffer;
Why must we all die?

Consider life's time span,
The challenge in space:
Consider the birth
Of the whole human race.

Was there really an Adam?
A woman called Eve?
A tree of great knowledge?
A snake to deceive?

Was mankind created
By an unchanging plan?
Or did chance forge the link
Between amoeba and man?

Does Loch Ness hold monsters,
A Blarney stone magic?
Can't life be more joyful
Instead of so tragic?

And what of the Piper
Who bedazzled, beguiled?
Did he make disappear
Every Hamelin-town child?

Will wishes come true
If you wish on a star?
Do rainbows give gold
If you follow them far?

What of history's greats—
Da Vinci, Saint Paul?
Of Mendelssohn's music
From Heaven's own hall?

What of Atlantis?
The Fountain of Youth?
What tale sings of legend?
What song rings of truth?

Ponder tall mountains
And ponder deep seas,
But when crises surround you,
Then fall on your knees...

And pray to the Father,
The Spirit, the Son;
Relinquish the heartache,
And peace will be won.

49.

50.

For prayer has the power
To erase question marks,
And to bring faith alive
In the spiritual darks.

Do miracles happen?
Did a babe become king?
In a Bethlehem stable
Did angel hosts sing?

Did shepherds abiding
In fields see a star
And hear the injunction,
"Go, follow it far!"?

Wise men today still
Acknowledge Him King,
And swear their allegiance,
Though no angels sing.

So, lawyer and doctor,
Scientist and actor,
Continue your questions;
It's the old human factor.

55.

56.

But when darkness surrounds you,
And life seems to deceive,
Just pray to the Father,
And ask to believe

In the God who created
Your questioning heart,
Then ask for His wisdom,
His joy to impart.

For He does have a story
For you to walk in,
A plan of salvation
To rid life of sin.

He strengthens, empowers,
With His wine and His bread,
As you come to His table
Your soul to be fed.

59.

So ponder, you poets,
Theologians, and all,
The mystery of seasons —
The spring and the fall.

Of stars in their heavens,
What lies under the sea?
Of genetics and bloodstreams —
What makes you and me?

61.

62.

Just why during childhood
Time creeps like a snail,
Yet when you're adult
Seems to fly and assail?

And what of sweet apples
That know when to fall,
Of babies and bulldogs,
Of things that appall?

How did history begin?
Will our food really last?
How will it all end—
With a choir or a blast?

LA.

And when, in a fetus,
Is a person first found?
Should I be cremated
Or just put in the ground?

And test-tubing babies —
Is it ethically right?
Are there really ghost things
That go bump in the night?

Do demons and devils
Abound in this place?
Do guardian angels
Enter our space?

How do frogs spring from tadpoles
And oysters make pearls?
How do boys become men,
While women were girls?

You may question in daytime
And all through the night
How ears really hear
And eyes call forth sight;

How some worms can crawl,
Then learn to wear wings;
How spiders can spin
Such gossamer things;

How the brain is divided
Into left and the right...
Of Einstein's relativity,
And Ben Franklin's kite.

71.

Who informs salmon
Their home is upstream?
What causes people
To sleep and to dream?

How do bears hibernate?
And geese find their way south?
Can we tame hurricanes
Or eliminate drought?

73.

74.

How do bulbs bring forth tulips,
And acorns, oak trees?
How can man boast of wisdom,
Yet spread war's disease?

What think you of Easter?
Did they lie and deceive
When they said "Resurrection!"
To all who believe?

Oh, I pray for you, friend,
As you question life so,
That one day you'll say
"Hey, I really don't know!

"It's your world, dear Lord,
In all of its glory!
I want to be yours;
Help me walk in your story."

Carolyn Huffman

" Often I ponder ... "

"... Sometimes I pray"

How this book came to be written ——

"God's other name is surprise!" How often I have heard my friend, John Claypool, declare this. And just as often I have seen these words fleshed out in my own life. My book, *Life Between the Questions*, represents one of these times.

Because of many reasons, mainly procrastination, I had not written professionally for about a year. Chuck, my husband, was most unhappy that I was neglecting my gift of writing. And I was experiencing a real restlessness in my soul.

About gifts . . . . I believe that we either use them or lose them. I dreaded picking up mine again, for I knew that the initial writing experience would be like walking through mud, very thick mud, and all uphill! With a prayer for God's guidance I began the discipline of writing with the hope that I would run out of "mud" before I ran out of endurance.

One night, after four months of diligently, slowly shoving one word in against another, I was awakened from a sound sleep. Creativity was exploding inside me like popcorn kernels. And it had nothing to do with the book I had been working on! That was the beginning of this book. For about a week I was consumed, and "pregnant" with the manuscript. Sometimes, I would have to pull off a busy street to write down the thoughts that insisted on being born!

When I finished writing my sixty-eight verses, I shared them with my husband. He is a very logical, practical, "left-brained" person, and I was half afraid he would find my efforts lightweight or silly. But, to my surprise, Chuck liked them! He said, "Carolyn, do you know what you have just written? This is an adult Dr. Seuss book! I see it being published along with illustrations."

The next morning my outspoken, pragmatic friend, Jack, called. Knowing he would be honest, I decided to read my manuscript to him and risk his opinion. And for a second time I was surprised. With no equivocation, Jack thundered, "Publish it!"

Over the next few months, I continued to be surprised by the way my little verses seemed to affect people. A young Californian, a songwriter friend of our daughter, Heather, read the manuscript and said, "I am stunned! How did your mother know all the questions I have been unable to articulate?" I gave a copy of the manuscript to a ninety-two-year-old friend who had been hospitalized. About a month later she showed Chuck the worn, battered pages saying, "These are the words that help keep me going."

How do I explain these reactions? I think these people's responses have to do with the fact that this book speaks to deep longings and needs all of us have. As my publisher remarked when he first read the manuscript, "This is where people are living their lives out ... between the questions."

Right from the start, I thought of my artist friend, Lu Ann Barrow, to illustrate the book. So I was very pleased when another friend, Keith Miller, read the manuscript and suggested, "Carolyn, there is an artist who paints the way you write. You both touch the inner child that all of us big folks still carry around with us. Get Lu Ann Barrow!" Fortunately for me, Lu Ann *was* able to do the illustrations, and they are everything Keith and I thought they would be.

This book starts out with the phrase, "Often I ponder,/Sometimes I pray." I hope it will inspire you to keep doing both. For I believe questions are very important. So often, discovering the right questions to ask becomes the preamble to finding the elusive answers to life. Processing questions also allows us to see that, in this life, some questions simply have no answers. But these questions are important, too, because they point us toward the One who is, after all, the real Answer to all our pondering.

Carolyn Huffman